The Invitational Christian

By Dave Daubert

Day 8 Strategies
Elgin, IL 60123

© Copyright 2017 by David Dennison Daubert

All rights reserved. No part of this publication may be reproduced, distributed, or transmitted in any form or by any means, including photocopying, recording, or other electronic or mechanical methods, without the prior written permission of the publisher, except in the case of brief quotations embodied in critical reviews and certain other uses permitted by copyright law. For permission requests, write to the publisher, addressed "Attention: Permissions Coordinator," at the address below.

Cover design and book layout done by Nate Daubert.

Larger quantities of this book are available at a discount. For information on purchasing bulk quantities for groups, contact the publisher at Resources@Day8Strategies.com for more information.

ISBN 978-0-9910621-1-9

Day 8 Strategies
1132 Morningside Dr.
Elgin, IL 60123
www.Day8Strategies.com

To contact the author send an email to: DDaubert@Day8Strategies.com

Table of Contents

Introduction		i
Chapter One	**A Changing World**	1
Chapter Two	**Why Should Anyone Come**	9
Chapter Three	**Quality Matters**	21
Chapter Four	**Knowing Our Story**	29
Chapter Five	**Address Their Fears**	39
Chapter Six	**Give Them Tools**	49
Chapter Seven	**The Importance of With**	59
Chapter Eight	**Following Up**	67
Postlogue		73

Introduction

This book is the result of a lot of angst within the church. I know about this angst, because I spend many of my waking hours thinking about and working within the church. While it is an exciting time to be the church, it is also a scary time to be the church. Most of the rules for being the church in our world are being called into question. Many of the rules are just plain changing. Some of the rules have already changed and no one told us, we just have to figure it out.

Not all of this is bad news. In fact, I am excited by the possibilities.

For too long the mainline church has relied on its social position to bring people to it. The result has been less emphasis on discipleship and all of the related things that disciples do. Church membership has become one hobby among many for a high percentage of our members. Often, it isn't even their most important hobby. As a result, the church has lost members, is aging, and is often demoralized.

Of course, there are people who see church life as a way of centering their entire lives as followers of Jesus. But many

Christians routinely set up their lives in ways that belie the fact that many other things compete for their allegiance. Many of those things actually get their first allegiance.

As a result, there has been a decline in church participation that people grieve but don't know what to do to change. They all too often simply wait, watch and hope.

This book is not long. This book is not complicated. But the chapters here are based on some solid, simple and practical things that every congregation needs to put into place in order to function better as Christ's ambassadors in this new time. In addition, this book takes into account feedback from the people who attend congregations that I know to be generally vibrant but where people are still learning to be invitational. As a result, the work is directly connected to people's experiences and feelings in the pews and in their daily lives.

I am thankful for the people at First Presbyterian Church of Elgin, IL; Pilgrim Lutheran Church of Chicago, IL; and St. Paul's Lutheran Church of Waukegan, IL. Each of these congregations had people who filled out surveys and shared their insights about invitation and why they do or do not invite people to join them in church life. Their input was invaluable.

I am also thankful for the people of Zion Lutheran Church in Elgin, IL where I have been privileged to serve as pastor for nearly fifteen years. The people there shared their thoughts about invitation, as well. But they have stretched and grown and changed in many ways during my time there as pastor. And they have stretched and changed and helped me grow as well.

My wife Marlene, a rostered deacon on our staff at Zion, is my strongest encourager and partner in both life and ministry. I am blessed to have her as my companion in life and thankful for the many ways that she has made me a better person.

And many thanks to Mandy Garcia, who served to edit the manuscript and helped me appear a bit more literate. Her work helped clean up my manuscript and likely made this book a better reading experience for those who pick it up.

This is not a final treatise on sharing faith and inviting others into life with Christ. It is a simple but solid foundation from which this work can begin and grow. I hope that as readers read this book, more ideas come to mind. If so, please contact me and share ideas and stories from your experiences.

All of us who are Christians know of God's love for us in Christ because of other people. I became a Christian because friends in my college dorm invited me to attend church. Because of them I was exposed to a way of seeing God in Christ that was gracious and life giving. It changed my life in many, many ways – far more than a brief paragraph can mention.

There are millions of people waiting for the same good news to impact their lives. Most of us know at least a few dozen of these folks pretty well. God is calling us to share the incredible message of Christ's love them and to then invite them into a life of faith as followers of Jesus.

I hope this book helps a few more of us to do that work a bit better.

Dave Daubert

1

A Changing World

If you are interested enough in inviting people to church to be reading this book, much of the material in this first chapter will likely be familiar. It is no secret that church life was once a centerpiece of North American culture and has slowly but steadily moved into the shadows. You may already know specific reasons for this shift, or you may simply "know" it intuitively because the congregation where you participate has been shrinking and aging.

There are many myths about Christianity and its golden age. For example, many believe that the United States was founded in order to be a Christian nation. While it's true that there were many Christians involved in founding the country, there were also those who were not only not Christian, but who opposed the involvement of any religious institutions in the work of becoming a nation. While most of the founders did believe in God in some way, their views and convictions were all over the map. They worked hard to acknowledge a shared belief in God and a conviction that the world had certain realities derived from God, but also to be clear that this new country would be an experiment in cultivating a national identity without any official religious expression. While Christianity was an important part of the backdrop, it was not included in the essence of what it meant to be an American.

That information is important, but historic. It provides a backdrop for the current downward trends of the last few decades.

More formative to the church in America was its rise in the aftermath of World War II. Christianity was the dominant religious force in the United States and it peaked during the 1950's when three things came together at the same time:

First, the triumph of our allies over Japan and Germany in World War II meant that the U.S. entered a time of great growth and prosperity. Soldiers returning home and the infusion of cash through things like the GI Bill meant Americans were rebuilding the economy. As they built homes and expanded the workforce, the demand for all new things to furnish their homes and offices increased. New technologies meant that owning cars and televisions became standard. Before the war, during the Depression, most people got by with less, but after the war there were new opportunities for everyone to have and produce more. America was in an expansion mode and the church was included.

Second, the post World War II environment featured the Cold War and the first competitive global environment developed with new technology. Radio and television began to broadcast new ideas and images directly into millions of living rooms, including images from the Soviet Union and Red China of life without God—an atheistic ("godless") world filled with enemies and danger. But against that evil stood America, a godly nation committed to good and everything that God wanted. The Pledge of Allegiance and American currency were modified to include explicit references to God. The Boy Scouts added a badge for "God and Country." Being religious was equated with being good and being American, and being a Christian held the weight of righteousness and civil respectability.

Third, the return of so many World War II soldiers and the impact of affluence meant that many new families were forming—all at the same time. Because modern birth control methods (especially contraceptive pills) didn't become readily available until the 1960s, families quickly grew and caused a "baby boom" that brought incredible numbers of children into society. Anything and everything that was needed to support them grew as well. As communities expanded, new schools were built and (you guessed it) churches built bigger buildings and educational wings. Many church facilities that were built in the 1950s and 60s featured cathedral-like sanctuaries and big educational wings. They expanded alongside everything around them.

But underneath all that expansion, trouble was brewing. Even during two decades of incredible growth in the church, the country was growing even faster, and the church began slipping in overall influence. Church involvement peaked as a percentage of the population in approximately 1950, and the percentage of Americans who actually belong to a church has been steadily declining since then. Even worse, the percentage of those who actually *participate* in church has been declining even faster. For over a half century—much of which was cloaked by the growth of the baby boom—the church has been gradually becoming less and less a part of the fabric of American lives.

By the time raw numbers made this reality obvious, the church was already much farther down the road to decline than it realized. Today, a relatively small percentage of Americans attend worship on a typical Sunday morning—somewhere between 12 and 16 percent, according to data provided by churches. That means that less than one in six people are in church on any given Sunday while others sleep, golf, shop, watch kids sports games, or any of a zillion other things. As a result, many of those big, beautiful churches built in the 50s and 60s have empty seats, oppressive utility bills, and vacant classrooms.

Even among those who regularly attend church the rate of attendance has changed. While those who considered themselves "active" or "regular attenders" in 1950 came to church every week, someone with the same self-understanding today may only attend one or two times each month. This means that a church's base requires more members to help a sanctuary feel "full" than it would have a few decades ago.

The impact? When people do attend (especially visitors), it can feel as though they are visiting a dying remnant of days gone by, rather than a vibrant expression of a community that follows Jesus.

As the church becomes more of a minority activity in our culture, the chances of connecting with those who are not in the church decrease as well. With less social orientation toward encouraging church attendance, people are less inclined to prioritize church in their busy lives. And as fewer people attend, fewer people are spending time with others in their congregation.

This is why congregations that believe that faith in Christ changes lives, and that participation in Christian community matters, will do well to train their members to invite others in.

Most congregational participants wish attendance was higher and that more people were involved. Many older folks grieve that young families and children are less a part of their fellowship of faith. But rarely do people who have not previously been part of church life consider visiting a congregation out of curiosity.

In my consulting work I have helped numerous congregations renew and become more vibrant. Assessments of that work have almost always been positive, and congregational leaders report that the work we did was extremely helpful. Energy is up. Community engagement is up. Members' sense of discipleship is up. Basic measures routinely show helpful and important outcomes. For this fact, I am extremely grateful—it keeps me doing what I do.

But I have also noticed that in many cases, strengthening a congregation hasn't led to the level of increased involvement that the church had hoped for, and I have been puzzled by why people who are more dynamic and vibrant in their faith don't invite others to join them. Inviting others in seemed like a natural and desirable response for a renewed and invigorated congregation, so how could I learn from this mystery and discern what was keeping people from doing so?

Pastors often wish parishioners would invite more visitors to attend with them. Parishioners often report liking their church and finding life, meaning, and hope there. Yet the average mainline churchgoer rarely invites others to attend.

Why?

The remaining chapters in this book are designed to explore that question. Why are dedicated participants not inviting others to take part in a vibrant, meaningful, congregationally based faith life? And based on what those issues are, how can we help change behaviors that have been internalized over decades and regain a more discipleship-based way of offering a life of faith and connection to Christ to others? Over the next few chapters we'll explore the components of successful invitation, and how it can change lives and increase congregational vitality.

For Reflection or Discussion

Scripture

Read 1 Corinthians 15:1-11. In this section Paul reminds the church of the death and resurrection of Jesus and the power that it has to bring life to those who believe. How does this message get communicated where you worship? How has it given you life?

Questions

Take time to reflect on these individually in a journal if you are reading this book alone. Or, if you are reading this with a group, use the following questions to discuss what the people in your small group are thinking as a result of this chapter.

* What in this chapter reminded you of some important idea or else made you think in a new way?

* As you think back as far as you can remember, what has changed about the place of church in the world around you?

* Does it surprise you that only about one in six people attend worship each week? If so, why do you think this surprises you? If not, what signs have you seen that cued you into this?

* How has participation changed in the congregation(s) you have been a part of? Think about age, ethnicity, and the numbers of people attending various aspects of church life. What shifts have you seen? What shifts didn't happen?

* What changes in practice has your congregation already implemented in response to the changing landscape around you? Which ones have helped you be more missional? Which changes have been just to survive in declining situations?

Prayer

God of the church, in Christ you have called us to be the body of Christ for the world. Yet, across our land the church is often struggling to be all that you are calling it to be. Help us to reflect on the changes in the world around us and be open to your call for the church to change in ways that make it more effective. Bless us with hopeful spirits and willing hearts and minds. In Jesus' name we pray. Amen

2

Why Should Anyone Come?

The first part of empowering people to become more invitational is by helping them articulate a "why" behind the invitation. The mere desire to help one's congregation is not usually enough and, biblically speaking, it lacks merit. There is little in scripture that points to simply growing the church's size as a goal in and of itself.

A healthy congregation has clear values and practices at the core of its identity. It has a shared life in a community where people of faith care for one another, share stories of God's work in their lives, pray for one another, and cultivate a meaningful and life-giving relationship with the world around them. They have a sense that God is alive and at work among them and through them. They aren't sitting back waiting for new people to attend—they are actively engaging a life of faithful service and discipleship.

Sadly, most congregations that are in decline are missing this dynamic faith life. Study after study has concluded: most of our congregations lack the required vibrancy to know and show why being part of a faith community matters. When visitors come, they often don't find what they came for

(God, and people who are attentive to God). They find a tired group of nice people who are hoping something will turn things around.

The Wrong Reasons

In the first congregation that I served, I quickly learned about the implicit "save the congregation" mindset that often intrudes our thinking. I include myself in that temptation. As a pastor, the need to sustain the congregation where I serve can seem like motive enough. But an encounter I had during my first year in my first parish taught me to keep my eyes open to this survivalist mindset and to reject it as a valid reason to look for new people.

I had just finished my first stewardship sermon. It was fall, and I had been in the congregation as its pastor for about six months. The small, struggling band of aging parishioners were saddled with a huge building. We had over 500 seats in a pillared, neo-gothic sanctuary with a huge balcony, a massive organ, and high sanctuary ceilings that were over four stories above the floor. We had 66 pews for an average of about 45 people each week. If you got bored during the sermon, you could lay down for a nap and no one would notice!

After worship that day, one of the long-time members of the congregation hung around to wait for me. A tall, stern man, he waited until I was the last person in the building before approaching me. He wanted to talk. He wanted to catch me off guard. He wanted us to be alone.

Stopping me on the steps and standing one step above me to emphasize his height and imply a position of power, he spoke. It was short and to the point and the only sentence I remember is etched in my mind, word for word: "Pastor Daubert, if you'd go out there and do some evangelism, then you wouldn't have to come after us for our money."

That was pretty clear. According to this man, the reason we needed new members was that we needed money. The more people we had, the more money we would have. In addition, the more others gave, the less we were expected to give. If we could recruit enough contributing church members, being part of the church could be less about our own discipleship and more about the ease of cruising on a big ship. In other words, the more people we had in church, the less need there was for us to be committed disciples of Jesus.

The need for more money is neither a gospel-based, nor an effective reason to invite others into the life of our congregation.

A second story from the same congregation:

During a board meeting we were discussing reaching out to our local community. White, working class people had once primarily occupied our neighborhood but over the last few decades had shifted significantly and become a lower-income, racially diverse community. The few white folks who remained were either aging or were Appalachian and had moved in from rural places looking for jobs in the city. Almost none of the new people looked much like the remaining members of the congregation.

This new reality inspired fear and animosity in our church leaders. Many had internalized that the church was doing exactly what it had done when the congregation was thriving in the 1950s and 1960s, so our dwindling attendance couldn't have been blamed on us. Obviously, there must be something wrong with the new people in our community. Finally, in a moment of tension during the meeting, someone blurted out what many were thinking: "I don't know why we are so worried about reaching these people. If they were respectable, they'd already be here!"

Can you hear the remnants of the 1950s and Cold War mindset discussed in the first chapter? Christianity was a sign of our goodness and righteousness as opposed to the ungodliness of our Cold War opponents. Good, respectable people were inside the church, and "they" were outside the church, so "they" must not be respectable. End of argument.

The belief that we are "good people" is also not good theology, gospel-based, or an effective reason for inviting people into the life of our congregation.

Overcoming "Why Not…" From the World Around Us

If the first two problems with why (or "why not") to invite others to church are based on internal issues, then a third comes from outside the church. As culture has become less "churchy," the default assumption that church is good has changed as well. In a bygone era, people had faith in the church, trusted it, and were generally predisposed to consider being part of it. But a decline in participation, a rise in church scandals around sexuality and money, a general perception of judgmentalism and hypocrisy, and simple benign neglect have reversed or removed that default assumption for many.

In fact, many people carry a lot of baggage about the church and want nothing to do with it. They have seen and heard enough. They have stories of being forced to go to boring Sunday school or being chastised for fidgeting in worship. They are so done with church. In fact, some are so done with church that not only have they not gone, they were raised by parents who didn't go either. For a very high percentage of young adults in America, church is simply "off the radar."

So why should anyone invite someone else to attend church? More specifically, why should you invite someone to attend your church?

The Best "Why"

For a congregation to be truly invitational, it must adopt and embrace two major reasons for inviting others to church.

The first reason is that the congregation itself matters and is actively participating in work that matters to God. This is where a clear identity (core values, guiding principles, mission priorities, etc.) is essential. Along with clarity, the connection between who you are and what you do must be established—people must feel that their congregation is a place that truly matters to God. To help determine who you are as a ministry and whether your congregation has articulated a mission identity, reflect on your purpose, principles, and priorities. (This kind of reflection is best done in a small group, rather than individually.)

Purpose: A healthy congregation has studied scripture, prayed, and discussed why it exists and what God might hope will happen as a result. A healthy congregation knows that the God we meet in Jesus is on a mission to love and bless the world. They know that God's desire is to work with people, not instead of them, and that they are part of Jesus' community of allies who serve as his hands, feet, and voice in the world. From this they are able to articulate a sense of purpose and a clear and consistent message about their commitment to furthering God's work and dream for the world.

Principles and/or values: A healthy congregation also knows which values and behaviors are most related to God's dream for their life together and their witness to each other and to those around them. They have discussed a vision of who they are at their best and decided what matters most about their identity in Christ. They know that their calling is not to simply wait and hope that this vision will come to fruition someday in the future, but to live it and pursue it in the present. And whether they articulate these as guiding principles or core values, a healthy congregation knows that they are accountable to making these indicators as visible as possible every time they gather.

Priorities: While there is a picture of the ideal church in many of our members' minds, it is most often a memory of something that was, rather than a commitment to what is or can be. This means that a healthy congregation has engaged God, their members, and community neighbors to discern what is most important. Not every good priority from 1965 is relevant today. Many of the most helpful things about a dynamic congregation emerge from the local context and sometimes aren't useful in a congregation only a few miles away. Congregations that are clear about what is most important can make a case for the work they do and are better able to invite others into that work. "Would you like to come to church?" is replaced by, "My congregation is working on _____ and I know you care about that. Would you be interested in helping?" You can hear the clarity and winsomeness in that already!

A congregation that knows why they exist, what they embody, and where to focus their energy is in a much different place than a congregation that continues doing business as usual. Business as usual is what got us here. It will take something else to change course and produce different results.

Because the congregations surveyed for this book have been through work in the areas of purpose, principles, and priorities, they all have some form of clarity about why they exist and what they value. The respondents' answers reflected this as they talked about doing the work of God, connecting people to God, creating supportive faith communities, and other things related to congregations with missional clarity. It was good to see this, as the congregations involved in the survey were chosen because they showed signs of effectiveness in these areas. At the same time, they were also chosen because they still identified barriers to regular invitation.

A second key answer to the question, "Why invite others to church?" is found in what is happening in the lives of participants. In a healthy ministry, people sense that it is life changing. The teaching, spiritual support and guidance, and the impression that being in the congregation will actually deepen their spiritual lives; all transform church into more than a social or religious activity. When people participate in congregational life, they feel more connected to the God who calls them, and they have more awareness of the intersection between their life and the work of that God.

The result is a sense of wholeness that transcends any given circumstance. It is a commitment to the things that matter most to God, even to the point of personal sacrifice and giving of time and energy. A vibrant congregation helps participants identify their involvement in the organizational church as only one expression of an entire life of discipleship that impacts their home, their work, the way they engage their neighbors—literally everything about who they are and what they do.

In addition, the result of engaging in life-changing ministry is a sacrificial spirit that helps congregants engage what matters most to God, rather than buying into the myth that being a Christian leads to an easier, more affluent life. Healthy congregations help people to be more loving, with all the costs associated with loving like Jesus, as they take up their crosses and follow Christ.

Respondents to the surveys used to shape this book often expressed answers that reflected this feeling of wholeness and fulfilling purpose. When asked what a new person would find by coming to the congregation, one of the answers was, "Knowing that God loves them where they are and the way they are. It is the start of new life." Another said, "You see the world differently through His eyes." Yet another said, "Adding meaning to their lives."

As one pastor said to me, "God has given us what we need to engage the cultural shifts that are happening all around us, but we haven't always been able or willing to develop the relationships needed to communicate and share with those around us." Studies show that people in general and younger adults in particular are looking for warmth, family, a place to unplug from technology, and a place where they can find answers to relevant questions in their lives. Those studies also show that Millennials are not overly interested in church life but are often interested in learning about Jesus. Many are curious about God and finding purpose and meaning in their lives. A congregation that is serious about helping connect others with God has something very powerful to offer.

Every congregation that is concerned about a lack of enthusiasm for invitation should seriously assess whether they truly believe that they matter to God and that they are a valuable part of God's work in the world. If the congregation lacks missional clarity or does not help people grow spiritually to be more like Jesus, then it lacks the central components of its calling and purpose.

If this is true for the congregation where you participate, you may want to push invitation to the back burner and refocus on foundational issues first. Being clear about why your congregation exists and how you encourage others in their spiritual journeys may unlock potential that will not only help you reach others, but renew the congregation's life together and the spiritual lives of those who already attend.

For Reflection or Discussion

Scripture

Read Acts 2:37-47. In the earliest days of the church they had to integrate thousands of new people into the church. Doing so meant establishing practices that created meaning, order and were life giving. What about your congregation is life giving? How is it lifted up and shared clearly in ways that allow new people to respond and participate?

Questions

Take time to reflect on these individually in a journal if you are reading this book alone. Or, if you are reading this with a group, use the following questions to discuss what the people in your small group are thinking as a result of this chapter.

* What about the material in this chapter made you think about something in a new way or else revisit something you had already been pondering?

* Does your congregation feel pressure to invite more now because of self-referencing things like a shortage of people, an aging congregation, or concerns about money? If so, which ones press you the hardest and why?

* Think about the key reasons why a congregation is a good place for someone to explore. There were two primary reasons discussed in this chapter:

  - Helping people be a part of the mission of God;

  - Deepening people's spiritual connections to God in ways that are transformational.

  Is either of these emphasized in the congregation where you worship? If so, how does this happen already? If not, what needs to happen to make this stronger?

* If someone new came into your congregation looking for God, where do you think they would be most likely to notice God's presence and work there?

* If someone new asked you, "How is God changing your life this week?" what would you say? If that same person asked, "How is this congregation joining with God in God's work right now?" what would you say?

Prayer

Amazing God, you are on the loose and bringing life all around you. If we open our eyes and hearts we can see the impact of your movement all around us and deep within us. Help us to be more aware of your work. Help us to be more open to your call to join with you in that work. Help our congregational life to reflect that in ways that are powerful and contagious. We pray this in the name of your Son, Jesus Christ, our Savior and Lord. Amen

3

Quality Matters

A recent study shows that people value meaningful sermons more than any other single aspect of congregational life. Worship also ranked high. Many congregants love their church and even their pastor, but are unsure if their love will translate to something that visitors will also love. This means that they are unlikely to invite a friend to church if the quality is not consistently high enough.

It may seem like a harsh statement but by definition, roughly half of all places are below average. This means that half of all congregations have below-average preaching. Half of all congregations have below-average worship. Half of all congregations' buildings are in below-average condition or filled with clutter. The list goes on. If you are below average in several things, this adds up to a not-very-good experience to invite others into. The fact that you love your church is important, but it may not be enough to give you the confidence to invite others in.

This reality should make all of us pause and take stock of what we are doing and how we are doing it. Taking an assessment of reality can be both eye opening and painful. What if we need to work at the quality of our sermons, even if we love the preacher? What if our worship and music aren't so hot, even though the organist has been our friend for decades? What if we all love to sing certain songs and grumble when a new song is added to the mix, only to realize that we need to be open to new music in order to better connect with those we are called to reach? What if we all like one another pretty well, but we aren't good at helping new folks penetrate our circles (which are often cliques)? What if we want new people to join us, but only it they're willing to adapt and become just like us?

People come to church to hear a word from God, experience a connection with God, and to build supportive and meaningful relationships with people who love God and each other. They aren't looking for a new clique—they have enough of those to tend to already. Show them God and that you care about God and they will be intrigued. Show them a below-average church and they will remember why they have been staying home all along.

Now a second truth: Average isn't working very well.

As we discussed in chapter two, typical congregations are shrinking and aging. It is no secret that people are not coming to church on their own or sticking around to be part of what we are doing. The truth is that 85 percent of mainline congregations maintain stagnant membership or are in decline. That means the pool of peers we are comparing ourselves to isn't setting the bar very high. In a world where everyone is drowning, settling for treading water may seem fine—until we get tired and start to sink. Then we realize that the "average" may not be all that good. In fact, we could be pretty far above average and still be in decline.

This is an awful lesson to learn. Members of the congregation where you participate might be working hard, innovating new ideas, and doing things better than they were in the past. Your congregation might even be above average when compared to other congregations—but all that still might not be enough. Ouch!

All of this matters because a dedicated church-goer might love their congregation, feel God is using them, and that they are spiritually growing by being involved, yet still be reluctant to share it with others. What we see in our long-term involvement may satisfy us, keep us motivated, and encourage us to give our resources to keep it going—but if things are not done well enough so that a friend visiting for the first time can overlook inconsistent practices or awkward gaps, we will not be inspired to invite them. We may love our church but be ashamed of the clutter in the halls, peeling paint in the sanctuary, or the musty smell emanating from the basement. What we are content to live with ourselves, we may not want company to see.

So, if you are clear about your sense of mission and can honestly discern that people are spiritually vibrant and growing, do an inventory of how well you actually carry out congregational life. If the preaching is so-so, encourage the pastor to get some continuing education. If the music is weak, make changes to make it the best it can be while remaining authentic to who you are. If nice members aren't able to genuinely welcome visitors when they come (something more than "Nice to meet you. I hope you'll come back."), work on it. If the building is dirty and cluttered, clean it up. No one wants to bring a friend into a messy church, no matter how much they may love it.

If you are like me, when you have company coming to your home you do some things to prepare. You sweep, mop, and vacuum the floors. You wipe down the counter and clean the bathrooms. You pick up stacks of mail and newspapers and either sort through them or put them out of sight. Then, when everything is how it should look, the doorbell rings and you smile as you welcome friends into a nice, clean home.

Although congregational life feels more like family, the reality is that our congregations also must be ready for company every week. The stuff we wouldn't let show if the bishop were coming to visit, we let show almost every other Sunday. Because we see it week after week, we know it's there but don't pay a lot of attention to it. If there is clutter, if a sermon isn't well prepared, if the music is so-so, it is all part of the norm and we are both used to it and forgive it.

In some ways, it has to be this way because we are a community of grace. (The quest for perfection can destroy a congregation as quickly as anything, so don't be too anal about getting everything perfect, especially all at once.) However, inadequacy or lack of confidence about what we have is a real issue. One survey respondent said, "Sometimes I think people are looking for more bells and whistles than we have— especially the younger generation." Statements like this may or may not be objectively true, but they are based on a perception that is real: congregants worry that the church they love may not appeal to someone they know.

This is why it is important to pay attention to quality—especially the quality of core things. Scripture tells us that each person we encounter represents Christ for us. The call of Jesus is that we represent Christ for them. While being gracious with reality is essential, it isn't an excuse for simply accepting and excusing mediocrity. Some things, like the long-term trajectory of worship or preaching, may take months or even years of ongoing attention to improve. But other things, like cleanliness and clutter, can be addressed and solved in a relatively short period of time.

Every Sunday is an odd mix of gathering "people who live here" with the notion that "company is coming." When you all know that everyone is paying attention to offering their best, most of the time, then everyone is more likely to feel confident that a guest will have a good experience of what it means to be part of the church.

In every congregation there are a few people who don't want the pastor to stop by, even by appointment. They love the pastor, attend church regularly, and are committed Christians, but their house is a wreck so they resist visitors. They love their home and are usually happy enough with how it is, but they don't want company—ever!

I have recently worked with a congregation where not only is the appearance of the facility an issue, but many members are invested in keeping it the way it is. Signs in the parking lot warn that non-members who park there will be prosecuted to the fullest extent of the law. Signs on the entrance imply that if you come in you should be sure to use the correct door and have a good reason to be there. When you get inside, too many signs overwhelm the visitor and the few important things are hidden. If a visitor braves going in, the sanctuary is beautiful but dark and a bit imposing. If they go downstairs, they'll enter a time warp to the 1950s. Old TVs are present in each room, along with a VCR for each one. Old paintings are stacked in many rooms—no place to be hung but too sacred to throw away. Stacks of books from decades ago are all around and boxes and stacks of clutter mark each room.

All of these things need to be addressed before any person outside the life of the church is likely to consider it. Some members know they need nothing more than a dumpster and some willing helpers. But others know that much of what would be thrown away is "priceless," and are horrified that today's kids don't want to watch a 25-year-old video on a 25-year-old TV. "There's nothing wrong with those things and our kids really enjoyed them when they were growing up," they say.

If certain aspects of your congregational life resemble this—literally in that the facility is a mess, or figuratively in that the quality is relatively inconsistent—work on it. Working to improve things will increase confidence in what you are inviting people into. It will also help you make a better impression when they come.

If you are ready for visitors when they come, they will be able to focus on the things that brought them in the first place instead of clutter or inconsistency. Being "company ready" allows guests to notice God's presence, and God is the reason we want others to join us in the first place.

For Reflection or Discussion

Scripture

Read Philippians 4:8-9. Paul lifts up the importance of focusing on things that are honorable and pursuing excellence. He knows that quality matters. How does your congregation's ministry put these exhortations into practice?

Questions

Take time to reflect on these individually in a journal if you are reading this book alone. Or, if you are reading this with a group, use the following questions to discuss what the people in your small group are thinking as a result of this chapter.

* Did anything in particular resonate with you as you read this chapter? If so, what was it and why do you think it connected with you?

* Think about the physical space at your congregation's facility. Perhaps even walk around the building (inside and outside) with open eyes. How does it look? What looks clean, focused and inviting? What looks cluttered, worn or dingy?

* Think about your congregational life and the quality of the actions. While it may be hard to discuss easily, talk about the quality of the preaching, music, education and other ministries within the life of the church. How strong are they? In what way would someone who is not already committed to church find them helpful and engaging?

* Think about times when you have visited other congregations. How was that experience for you as a visitor? Do you remember being impressed by anything you experienced? Do you remember being frustrated by anything that happened?

* If you could change one thing about how you "do church" now, what area of church life would you improve in order to strengthen the quality of the experience and visitor might have?

Prayer

God of all peoples, you call us to show your presence in our life together in ways that honor you and show your goodness to all we meet. Help us to pursue excellence in all that we do so that our building, our ministry and our life together show how deeply committed we are to loving you. Where we need to change what we do and how we do it, help us to do so with both courage and love. We pray in the name of Jesus Christ, our Lord and Savior. Amen

4

Knowing Our Story

In chapter two we discussed the importance of helping congregations know why they exist and how that reason relates to what God is doing in the world. It is my belief that church has nothing to offer if it doesn't offer the God we meet in Jesus. That God is creative and formed us and everything that exists. This is the one generic truth about God that is agreed on by almost everyone who believes in God, regardless of tradition.

What makes Christianity unique is that the same God who made the world continues to be involved in the world. We hear the word "Immanuel" to describe Jesus as, "God with us." It is our belief as Christians that the God who made the world has come into the world, lovingly engaged it, suffered death at the hands of the world, and been raised from the dead to announce the incredible persistence of God's love toward us, no matter what. That God works through the Holy Spirit to inspire us and promises that Christ will be with us in all things and for all times. This is not only a story about something that happened long ago—it is an ongoing story that started before creation and continues in our individual and collective lives to this day. God is up to something amazing and Christians are given insight and invitation into it.

This means that if our congregations are working well, we are helping each other see and make sense of how God is at work in our lives. But at almost any mainline congregation, the typical Sunday morning conversation doesn't usually include much about God. Listen and you will find that conversationalists often sound more like secular humanists than followers of a living God: weather, sports, family, and other generic topics are the center of attention. Any of these subjects could have a faith aspect—all of life involves God—but the chitchat filling our fellowship halls sounds not too different from that of a coffee shop on a weekday. If a visitor comes to church to find out what God might be up to in his or her life, they will all too often find people who haven't wrestled with that very question themselves.

This reality appears to not only impact visitors, but it is one of the reasons why members attend less in the first place. In a culture that is "spiritual but not religious," we have too many congregations that are "religious but not spiritual." That disconnect means that our souls crave something that we aren't getting. Our own spirits are drying up. As a result, it never crosses our mind to share it with someone else. And when a guest does come, they are often disappointed to find that the one thing they thought they would find in church was the one thing that seemed most clearly missing.

I once started to discuss faith stories with members of the congregation where I serve and afterward a woman came up to me and said, "You know pastor, I don't think I have a faith story."

Of course, she did have a faith story, but she had been raised in ways that encouraged her to think of her church activity as the focus, rather than her daily life. Her sense that she was on a spiritual journey, or her awareness of how God had shaped or accompanied her had never been cultivated. Years later, she now speaks about God's involvement in her story much more naturally and clearly, but that shift required practice and intentionality.

This lack of awareness is not unusual in many mainline congregations. Many people who have spent their lives committed to the church have done very little to connect their church involvement to the wider involvement of God in the rest of their lives. As a result, these folks often have difficulty engaging other people's stories in ways that illuminate how they see God at work in anyone else's life. This reality is increasingly significant because more and more people report that they wouldn't come to church out of religious impulse, but would consider it if church nurtured their spiritual hungers.

In general, this desire to be spiritually fed is true across all ages, but notably more so in younger generations. Data shows that approximately one in three young adults have no connection to religious institutions, and most of the remainder who do have some connection is not very active. But the same studies also show that these young adults are not disinterested in God—they simply want to understand how God connects to their lives and don't see church as a place to cultivate that understanding. This means that in order to take the church seriously, these individuals need your congregation to be a place where spiritual journeys are acknowledged and spiritual stories explored.

To encourage this behavior, congregations need to do the following things well:

Preaching: In general, pastors in mainline traditions have been taught to discern what the scripture text meant in its time and context. This has involved excellent training in biblical languages, history and archaeology, systematic theology, and a good understanding of issues and culture of the world of biblical times. Pastors are often experts and very good at sharing theological insights, explaining what the text was about, and why the author wrote the material in a certain way, etc. All of this information can help people today have a better understanding of the things Jesus and his followers did, and the world in which they lived.

But very few people come to church primarily to discover these historical details. This is not to say they are unimportant and can't be interesting in a sermon—they certainly can! But good preaching does not tell what happened as a destination; it tells what happened as a starting point. People do not come to hear that Jesus did something centuries ago, they come to encounter the living Christ today. They do not come to hear that Jesus saved, healed, or taught someone else a long time ago. They come to be saved, healed, and taught by Jesus now.

In order for people to discover their faith story, they first need to understand and experience that the gospel is not merely a point of fact from history, but a reality that grounds the present. Likewise, Jesus is not a person documented by history. Jesus is our crucified and risen Lord and Savior who is at work in the lives of people today.

This means pastors need to cultivate an awareness of the

living God in their own lives and communicate it in their preaching. They also need to use present tense verbs to describe what God is currently doing, rather than past tense verbs to document what God did long ago. Where stories can be told without embarrassment or violating confidentiality, stories of real people will help others discover examples of God's work in their own lives as well.

Conversations and Storytelling

Conversations need to be reshaped in the church so that people can share with each other their experiences and understanding of God and God's work. If members come to church and only talk about the same old things week after week, it demonstrates that faith adds nothing to the conversation. Pastors often implicitly encourage congregants to believe this by our lack of guidance—we allow default conversation topics to be things that are less than God's work around us. Rather than raising the bar, we settle for sociable, and the result is a pleasant death in all too many cases.

A healthy congregation encourages people to move the sermon from the pastor's lips to the lips of the people. If the sermon was about a certain aspect of our faith life, my hope is that participants discuss with each other where they've experienced it in their own lives. How have we wrestled with it? Where have we experienced God in it? One way we encourage this conversation in the congregation where I currently serve is by using a projector and slides during worship. The welcome screen always has a faith question related to the message for the day for attendees to consider as they prepare for worship. The goal is to provide content for conversation about faith and where they see God in their lives. The number of people who talk to me about that question each week often amazes me.

Being conscious about this shift in conversation will change the curriculum for education—both for adults and children. It is not enough to only learn about Jesus. Our role is to help people encounter Jesus. Helping our members engage Christ and find ways to articulate those encounters will strengthen and even transform their faith lives. It will also give their walk with God a dynamism that will be contagious and more likely to be shared. If we want to invite people to something more than a religious club, ensuring that our members are aware of and able to share their understanding of God is essential.

Finally, there are practical ways to help people reflect on their journeys and make sense of their lives. Starting with a theological framework can help people have the tools and lenses they need to discern. It also prevents conversation from degenerating into purely subjective tripe. (You probably don't want too many stories about being late for work and getting all green lights to dominate the sharing time!)

Making a timeline of key life events (good and bad) can be a starting point. Then encouraging reflection on what happened and how the individual experienced God in those events can be helpful. Journaling about these events is often a way to deepen understanding and give people the space and permission they need to reflect and see things in a new way. Then, providing judgment-free space for people to share their stories and what they understand about God is also important. This means covenanting that in that space, participants will listen respectfully, not challenge or one-up each other, and simply hear stories as fellow travelers trying to make sense of God and life together.

If stories are deemed helpful to a larger audience, worship planners can make space for brief testimonies or a video of the storyteller during worship or other gatherings. Listening to stories of others helps us to see that we all have a story to tell.

Spiritual Practices

One healthy trend in the church is the growing awareness that cultivating a spiritual life is a core component of being a Christian. Whether a person comes from a Roman Catholic background and is immersed in a traditional parish, or attends a large, evangelical mega church, one thing is consistent: Leaders in all traditions are discovering that teaching people faith practices and how to put them to use is vital.

This makes sense. Ancient traditions emerged from the early church as desert fathers and mothers shared their practices and taught followers how to focus and experience God in their lives. These traditions were shaped in various ways over the centuries by Celtic practices—teaching from St. Benedict, St. Ignatius and others—and by various Protestant teachers. Some traditions focused more on inner life, scripture, or other places of entry into a connection with a living God.

These deeper practices were often seen as being for more serious disciples or those with religious callings like pastors, priests, monks, and nuns. The result was an implication that a vibrant spiritual life was only for certain people. The rest of us would simply be blessed by whatever those "set-apart" disciples taught us, and God remained the special possession of a few, a curiosity for everyone else. And while the Protestant Reformation emphasized that all Christians have a prayer life available to them, countless studies show that while many people do pray, the vast majority aren't sure they are doing it right or are unclear about why they are doing it.

It stands to reason that those who believe that God is active and engage in the world would like to be connected to that work. Teaching disciples how to read scripture individually, or to practice lectio divina alone or in small groups, can help the yellowing old pages of a Bible come alive. Instructing individuals in the Ignatian practice of reflecting on the day to notice where God was at work can turn a bad day into a discovery of gratitude. Helping worshipers to meditate, contemplate, and listen for the voice and guidance of God can open whole new understandings of prayer. Introducing others to prayer walks and labyrinths can help those who have fidgeted for far too long to find new life and energy in their prayers by adding movement. Journaling can be a chance for participants to step out of their lives and into God's presence. The list goes on and on.

Congregations that want their members to know their individual faith stories will do well to help them regularly and intentionally spend time with God. Doing this work in one-to-one conversations, small groups, and educational time can change how members in your congregation see God in their own lives. It can renew their understanding of their personal stories and journeys, and it can excite them in ways that inspire them to share with others. When that happens, invitations are just around the corner.

For Reflection or Discussion

Scripture

Read John 1:29-34. John the Baptist has a clear way of telling his story and how he came to know Jesus as the one who brought him life. It is short and to the point – almost an elevator speech. What is the basis for his story? How does it help you think about how to articulate your faith story better?

Questions

Take time to reflect on these individually in a journal if you are reading this book alone. Or, if you are reading this with a group, use the following questions to discuss what the people in your small group are thinking as a result of this chapter.

* Did anything in this chapter touch you in some way that made you think? Made you cringe? Made you wonder?

* Think about your own faith story. When was the last time that your congregation provided an intentional place for you to share that story or to listen to someone else's faith journey?

* If you were to lift up four things in your life that you connect directly with God's involvement in your life, what things would you mention? How would you describe them as things God was involved in – what did God do?

* What spiritual practices do you practice on a regular basis? How do they help you stay connected to God?

* If you are in a group, take time to go around the circle and have everyone share an answer to the following question: "What has God done in your life in the last day for which you are thankful."

* What spiritual practices does your congregation emphasize and how do they provide training and/or encouragement for you to learn to incorporate them into your life? If the practices are helpful to you and others, how could you share them? If this needs attention, how would your congregation begin to deal with spirituality education more effectively?

Prayer

God of new life, you are moving in the world around us and you are involved in our lives. Help us to see your fingerprints on the patterns of our lives. Give us eyes to see you working in the world around us. Give us alert minds and thankful hearts that allow us to be filled with insights and gratitude for your work in our lives. Help us to find ways to be more open to you and closer to you each day. And help us to share the life we receive from you with others. We lift this to you in the name of Jesus. Amen

5

Address Their Fears

One of the main reasons that mainline Christians say they won't invite people to church is that they are afraid, and research for this book shows that this fear is not simply a cop-out—it is real. People are genuinely nervous about invitation.

If you're a leader, this may baffle you. Inviting someone to church doesn't seem life threatening, so what are they afraid of? Members seem happy enough with the church, so why are they afraid to invite others to join them?

Fears come in many forms. Some members know that fewer people attend church these days, so they fear rejection. Some know that fewer people are religious, so they fear being seen as weird. Some know less about the faith than they wish they did, so they fear seeming stupid. Each of these fears has been cultivated over years of reinforcement—much of which has been passive by neglecting to address the issue.

Other church members have expressed the notion that inviting people to church is best left to professionals. Of course, the average "professional" spends most of his or her time with church people or in the church office, so they often lack opportunities to share their faith. And truth be told, many "professionals" share the same fears as laity. In other words, we are all more in the same boat than we should be.

This means that leaders who want their congregants to be invitational need to directly address these fears. In preaching and teaching, these subjects should be raised, and hope and vision for something other than feared outcomes should be lifted up. (Evidence shows, for example, that many who are not involved in a congregation would attend if invited by someone they know and trust, which directly counters the fear of rejection.)

It is important to find out what prevents your members from inviting in order to address those barriers. This is an important step toward freeing your congregation to be more invitational, so let's walk through the most common fears and see how we might overcome at least some of their anxiety.

Fear of Rejection

The fear of being rejected is quite real and, of course, some invitations to attend church will be turned down. A good starting point for this fear is to acknowledge that not every invitation to our faith community will be accepted. And some guests who do come will not come back. So there is always a risk of feeling rejected. Help each other to accept that reality.

At the same time, study after study shows that while not all Americans are attending church or even interested in attending, there is a significant group of those who will attend if invited, and who show remarkable spiritual curiosity.

For example, in the recent Pew study that showed that 30 percent of all young adults have absolutely no connection to religious life (the highest percentage in history), it also showed that the majority of those same people were spiritually interested and longing for meaning, purpose, and spiritual vitality. Even among the least churched generation in United States history, the openness to saying "yes" was still present.

The likelihood of an invitation being accepted depends on its source. A random invitation from a door-knocker may not seem attractive, and these folks may have been turned down many times. But when one individual authentically connects with another, trust levels go up, so the better we know the person we are inviting, the more likely we are to be taken seriously. That means an honest invitation with integrity will sometimes receive a "yes." Rejection is not the only outcome.

Fear of Fanaticism

Another risk to invitation that church members often list is that, "If I invite someone to church or into religious life in any way, they may think that I am a fanatic." First, if you are a participant in mainline church life and fearful of the things listed in this chapter, the risk of being viewed as a fanatic is truly quite small. In fact, if concern about being viewed as a fanatic is on your list of worries, the odds are that you can stop worrying about it because, by definition, most fanatics couldn't care less about what other people think about them.

Part of this fear comes from a lack of role models. Most people have only seen evangelists on their porch who have seemed unconcerned about them or been pushy, fanatical, or judgmental. One person shared it this way: "I am worried about perception. I have been made so uncomfortable by pushy, judgmental people who need to mention God or Jesus in almost every sentence and tell me what I should be doing." Another was more concise: "I don't want to be seen as a Christian whack job."

In survey responses for this book it was clear that "being judgmental" was seen as a risk, fanaticism should be avoided at all costs, and that it was safer to do nothing than to cross a line where participants feared being seen as rude. Having articulated this, simply being gracious and courteous can alleviate many of these risks.

For starters, sharing why your faith matters to you or how you have experienced God, spirituality, etc. can give you a base from which to share. This creates a platform to make somewhat reasonable connections between your story, their story, and the invitation to experience something that is important and meaningful to you. Conversations like this will help things seem less obtuse and more authentic.

Second, being open to "no" is essential. Some survey participants were worried that they might get sucked into a debate or be seen as argumentative, but being ready to graciously receive any response lessens that outcome. If you share an invitation that is turned down, accepting the "no" without pressing allows your invitation to have merit while honoring their willingness to accept it or not.

But another key is to not assume that "no" means "never." Too often, members of mainline congregations allow their fears of being seen as pressing to force them to overcompensate. In the end, they seem half-hearted in their invitations and often describe behaviors that indicate that they may have given up too easily.

When friends in college first invited me to worship many years ago, I said, "no." They didn't press and they remained gracious. But they also said, "OK. Maybe some other time." They then politely and graciously asked again, and again. I never had the chance to view them as fanatics as they were always open to my willingness to come or not. But they did not simply give up and ignore this aspect of my life. They knew how to be caringly persistent without ever risking fanaticism. The outcome was life changing for me.

Fear of Harming a Good Relationship

The popular saying, "If it ain't broke don't fix it," often reigns in mainline church practices. We like to settle for adequate and leave well enough alone. This can permeate many aspects of our church life, and the practice of invitation is no exception.

This means that if we have a friendship with someone who is not part of a faith community, we are tempted to leave it that way. After all, we like each other and are getting along well right now. One survey responder shared the fear that, "Perhaps they will become standoffish from then on." Another simply said, "Changing our relationship." Why risk changing something that is going so well?

Risking the harm of a good relationship is perhaps the

most understandable of all the common fears. Leaving well enough alone is certainly easy and the safest route. It often takes little energy to keep things going smoothly.

At the same time, one definition I've read describes a friend as "someone who sees my foolishness and does not declare it to be a permanent condition." In other words, real friendship involves risk and vulnerability. Sometimes we strain the relationship, but to commitment to and work on the relationship can make it stronger. Many of our "friends" are merely acquaintances with upgraded labeling. We only improve that status if we risk some movement.

At the other end of the spectrum is the reality that a polite, gracious invitation to attend church is not really all that risky. If we invite a friend to attend with us and they decline, the odds are good that when we see each other over lunch next week, little will have been harmed in the relationship. In fact, the very act of inviting may express a level of friendship that had previously gone unnamed. That fact alone may have a positive impact even if the person never attends anything at your church.

Fear of Appearing Stupid or Foolish

Perhaps because mainline churches have taken spiritual growth and discipleship for granted for so long, many of our people seem frightened of the fact that being asked to talk about faith implies a certain mastery of content. Survey participants listed fears like, "I might not have the right answers to their questions," and "Not being able to answer enough questions."

When asked in the survey, many people were able to express their faith in strong, clear, and simple terms, but that fact seemed lost on them when they were asked why they were still afraid. In addition, participants who clearly demonstrated a sense of God's claim, love, and work in their lives often expressed concern that what they knew was not enough. If anything should cause church leaders to refocus their priorities, it's that many of our most active members feel inadequately prepared to talk about scripture and their faith.

This needs to be alleviated in two ways:

First, people need to be encouraged and supported in the things that they do know. Some of what members "don't know" is actually a lack of confidence and not at all related to content, so where strong faith exists, it should be celebrated. With few exceptions, people who don't attend church are not going to start interrogating those who do with detailed biblical and theological questions. They will be more interested in a clear and genuine faith that is humbly shared with enthusiasm.

Second, there is a genuine side of this fear that will benefit from long-term attention. Leaders will do well to help people think about clear ways to talk about the basics of faith. Providing opportunities to talk about what they believe and how they understand the Bible will help members gain language and confidence. This process is not a quick fix, but will change the conversations that congregations have together and help to alleviate the fear of appearing foolish.

Fears are real and cannot be dismissed by simply telling someone not to worry. At the same time, discussing fears and processing them carefully can help congregants deal with or even alleviate them completely. Taking time to work through this chapter and discussing it with others will be likely to be well worth the time. The results will be that fears are addressed and people are more confident. With that in mind, let's move forward to the next chapters and look at some very practical things to help members succeed in invitation.

For Reflection or Discussion

Scripture

Read Luke 1:26-38. Mary encounters the angel who tells her that God has an amazing task for her to do. Her initial response is fear (seems natural enough in this situation!). But the angel urges her to overcome her fears and be a part of what God is going to do. How could reflecting on how God can use you help you overcome your fears and anxiety about inviting others?

Questions

Take time to reflect on these individually in a journal if you are reading this book alone. Or, if you are reading this with a group, use the following questions to discuss what the people in your small group are thinking as a result of this chapter.

* What did you connect with most easily in this chapter? Why did that connect with you? Or, did anything catch you by surprise? If so, what surprised you?

* Think of a time(s) when you could have shared your faith or extended an invitation to someone but didn't. How did you feel? What prevented you from speaking up or inviting them?

* In this chapter there were four top answers to things that people said inhibited their ability to invite others (fear of fanaticism, fear of rejection, fear of harming a good relationship, fear of appearing stupid or foolish). Which of the issues in this chapter do you experience most often? How do you process these feelings? What do you think would help you to overcome them?

* How does your congregation talk about things that make people nervous or afraid? What would help bring these fears into the open and allow people to process their emotions in ways that could empower them to act more confidently?

Prayer

Mighty God, you have more strength and power than anything that exists. You promise to love us and be with us as we go – we are not alone or apart from your strength. Yet we fear so much and then fail to carry out the work you call us to do. Calm our fears and grant us the confidence and the strength to do what you call us to do, so that others may know what we know: that you are an amazing, loving and life giving God. We pray this in the name of your Son, Jesus Christ, our Lord and Savior. Amen

6

Give Them Tools

One key to invitation is the presence of... invitations. That may seem obvious but almost no congregation actually has them.

I have a friend who worked for years as a marketing executive for a large, multinational company. While he was there he felt called to become a pastor, so he studied and trained and when he turned 50 he retired and became a full-time pastor.

My friend was called to a large African American Baptist Church that was over 100 years old when he arrived as their senior pastor. The congregation had a long and proud history. They knew who they were and who they weren't. Attendance each week was slightly under 100 people for worship.

I have seen many congregations like my friend's over many years consulting. They are often solid, but have difficulty changing. They have a lot of experience being who they are and they like it. While they may, on the surface, want to grow, underneath there are all sorts of factors that hinder growth.

Fifteen years after my friend became their pastor, this congregation now has nearly 1,200 people in worship each week. They have built a new sanctuary and still need to send television feeds into the fellowship hall because the later service is often too full to accommodate everyone. The congregation is vibrant and makes as much of a positive impact in the community as any other congregation—white or black, Protestant or Catholic.

When I have been blessed to sit at his feet, my friend tells me some of the things that he has done to make this growth possible. I don't want to make it sound like every congregation should grow in the same way or expect these same results, but there are some things that are simply common sense and, for the most part, few mainline congregations are doing.

First, the congregation provides invitations for members to use on a regular basis. They are printed in color on quarter-page cards and distributed every three months. The invitation is redesigned four times each year in order to keep it fresh and encourage new invitations to be passed out. When the invitations are distributed to the congregation, there is also a motivational reminder about how to use them and to encourage people to do so. And they do.

Second, special invitations are also printed for major events in the church year. These include Christmas, Easter, and other things that you would expect, but there are often special schedules or extra services as well. These invitations are capitalizing on the fact that many individuals are often more alert to the Church's story during these times, even if they are uninvolved in the life of a congregation—it is pretty hard to slip through Christmas in our society without hearing something about the Christian story!

Third, when a family has a baptism, they meet with the pastor to prepare. As part of the preparation, my friend asks them to share six names and addresses of supportive friends of the family. He then sends individual cards to each of these friends by snail-mail, inviting them to come and be supportive on this important day. He admits that some people have occasionally resisted. But he usually wins them over and the result is that, on these special days, additional people come and see and hear about the work of the church and the message of the gospel. This can be a new beginning for some. After all, you can't come twice until you've come once.

Congregations may also find that business cards are an easy way to equip members for invitation. Have a thousand cards printed with your congregation's purpose and principles, or mission, vision, and values on one side, and contact data (name, address, phone, website, etc.) on the other. Give each member five cards and ask them to use them. Teach the congregation that when opportunities come up, they can simply pull a business card out of their purse or wallet, say a little something they find meaningful about the congregation's role in their lives, and give their friend or colleague the church's card. This may or may not include a concrete invitation, depending on the circumstances, but it is an excellent way to ensure that intermediate opportunities are not missed.

It is a clear fact that church members who have tangible reminders and cues are more likely to take action. In addition, the presence of a concrete invitation can help someone feel grounded and more in control, which is important when we recognize that many members of congregations are genuinely afraid of inviting others into faith life. Providing concrete tools can alleviate many fears that people carry.

Another set of tools for healthy and invitational congregations is on the web. While a good web presence is no substitute for an invitational culture, it can certainly help. Web tools provide a way to support the practice of invitation as well as one more vehicle for those invitations to occur.

One place to start is the congregation's website. There are more than a few people who will want to check out what it is that they are being invited to before coming. This is true of people who are thinking about accepting an invitation, as well as those who have said, "yes." They often want to check out the church website to find out what they are getting themselves into before they visit.

A good website is clear, simple, and up-to-date. This is more challenging than it sounds—I have seen way too many websites that still have ads for Vacation Bible School several months after it has ended! Many congregations have websites that are far more complicated than they need or can manage. While it may be entertaining to look at the complex websites of mega churches, remember that maintaining a clear, friendly, and accurate site is most important.

A good site features worship times, directions, and key information in a place where first-time website visitors can easily find them. Remember, a guest may only look once, so make sure they see things that pertain to visitors first. Too many congregations use their website to communicate with members and, in the process, overlook concerns and curiosity of web lurkers, so be sure that your site meets the eyes of non-members first.

In addition, a good site has useful information and content that changes relatively often. The adage that websites are the new Yellow Pages can be deadly. How often have you looked up an organization in the Yellow Pages and proceeded to regularly return to look at their ad? Not often, I'm sure! A website is not a Yellow Pages ad. It is a relational portal to connect with people. That means pictures, upcoming events, seasonal changes, special services, etc. need to be shifting on the site routinely, and this information needs to be easily noticed when a person checks in.

Next, consider a weekly blog. This is a great chance to do some online teaching and entice readers to come back and see what you've posted since last week. Building an email list of people who want to read your blog allows for you to share ideas with others in a safe way. (Be sure to record email addresses of visitors early!) Teach members to forward links to the blog or share new posts on social media, both of which are good starting points for conversation.

Another great idea that has proven to be helpful is recording the sermon and posting it on the church's website each week. Podcasts are becoming increasingly easy to produce, and they are one of the most convenient ways to encourage potential visitors to explore the congregation. For example, say one week the sermon is on a topic that connects with a member in a particular way. That member thinks a friend might benefit from hearing it, so they send a link to the sermon along with a personal note. That member has now introduced a friend to the congregation in a noninvasive way, and has laid the foundation for invitation.

An added bonus to podcasting is that a new post each week keeps your website fresh with new content, giving those who have found it a reason to come back again. And a collateral benefit is that it is a way to keep less active members connected. If someone misses worship and others are paying attention, they might send a note that says, "We missed you this week. Hope you are OK. If you need anything, please let me know and I'll try to help. Here's a link to this week's sermon. Hope to see you next week." Because faith is a communal reality, people often fall away and need to be re-invited. Things like a podcast and intentional connection can help to invite people back before the road home gets too long.

Social media is another chance to expand the congregation's sphere of influence and contact. Facebook, Twitter, and Instagram currently dominate church social media, but the reality is that there are increasingly diverse platforms for sharing and connecting with people. A decade ago the list would have included MySpace, and that platform is now nearly invisible! A good social media strategy allows for people to learn about events or information and then share them with others. In this way, someone you know may read your congregation's blog or listen to a sermon on a podcast. These things may touch them in ways that inspire them to connect further, or perhaps to share with others. Thanks to the internet, people you will never meet or even hear of may see something from your congregation.

It is essential to emphasize that social media is a tool to help congregations invite. These platforms are not an invitational strategy by themselves. In fact, many congregations have websites, Facebook pages, and Twitter accounts with little impact. A good online profile will not alter the future of a congregation that lacks clarity of purpose, vibrant ministry, or where people have little sense that God is real and active the world and their lives. Simply having a social media account does not equate to using it effectively. The old saying, "less is more," pertains here. Don't open up accounts on multiple social media platforms and use them erratically and poorly. For active social media users, that will reflect worse on your congregation than not having the accounts at all.

Also remember that an online message that implies life and vibrancy where there is none will ultimately cause more problems than good. Visitors who come expecting one thing and find another will not be happy. In addition, because many people who visit a congregation are not exploring only your church but religion itself, they will conclude that church is not for them. If they are exploring faith in general, these visitors will not try a different congregation next week. They will say, "I tried the Church. It wasn't ready for me." And they will often give up and remain disconnected. We have a moral obligation to be positive but authentic, invitational but honest.

It can be tempting to assume that an online presence is strategy enough. It feels relevant, connected to the times we live in, and safe—we can hide behind a screen and feel confident that we have done something. Perhaps it will bear fruit, but the truth appears to be that online invitations are not nearly as effective as person-to-person invitations made with spoken words, preferably face-to-face.

I was at a community organizing meeting a few weeks ago and the presenter said that his 30 year old daughter had become irritated about the quality of prison food during a volunteer effort and decided that women in prison deserved better meals. She wanted to organize people to lobby for improved meals, and though she lacked an organizational base to work from, she had lots of friends online. She asked her dad, a professional organizer, for help, and he told her to join a church. She needed to interact with people face-to-face if she was going to make a difference.

A bit put off and frustrated, she pressed her dad and he agreed to help her. She planned a morning action before work so that those who ran the prison would encounter a demonstration in front of their offices when coming to work. It would require inviting friends and colleagues to join in the protest by showing up at 7 a.m. to demonstrate.

The day of the protest arrived. The woman's dad had invited people face-to-face and found 25 people who had agreed to come. She had reached out online, set up a Facebook event, and had 10 people say they would be there. All 25 of her dad's people showed up, and none of the online commitments came through. She was crestfallen.

But this novice activist also learned something important: online relationships all too often lack the accountability to follow through. It is easy to say "yes," sign a petition, or do many things with a mouse-click. It is quite another to actually set your alarm, get out of bed, and show up.

These comments are not meant to slam social media or discourage people or congregations from using it—social media is certainly useful and important. But it is also important to be clear about what these platforms can and cannot do. In reality, it is rare when an interaction with someone you know only online has the same depth as a face-to-face interaction with someone with whom you have spent significant time.

If you want your congregation to invite, provide them with tools for invitation—whether tangible or electronic. In the end, both the physical tools and online tools are useful and important. Neither are magic remedies, but they do make a big difference.

For Reflection or Discussion

Scripture

Read 2 Timothy 1:3-7. This exhortation comes in a letter – one of the tools used in the early church to make connections. How does this letter strike you in its tone? In what ways does this resemble things that your congregation produces? In what ways is it different? Anything you might take from thinking about this?

Questions

Take time to reflect on these individually in a journal if you are reading this book alone. Or, if you are reading this with a group, use the following questions to discuss what the people in your small group are thinking as a result of this chapter.

* As you read this chapter, which things stood out for you and why?
* Reflect on the basic need for members to have things that they can share with others (brochures, cards, newsletters, etc.) in an ongoing way. What things does your congregation already provide for people to carry with them and share?
* Think about the chances to invite people to something special. What tools does your congregation provide for invitations to be easily made?

* As you assess the things in questions 2 and 3 above, what new idea(s) should you congregation consider implementing as next steps in doing a better job at this?

* Look at or reflect on the social media and web site for your ministry. Do they exist? Are they well-used and kept fresh and dynamic? Do they reflect well on the congregation and its ministry in a way that is also honest and authentic?

Prayer

Loving God, you have come to us in Christ and empowered us to believe and experience life in Jesus' name. Give us the desire to share the good news, the opportunities to bear witness to the work of Christ in our lives, and the things we need to do it well. Strengthen our ministry in ways that prepare us to always be ready to give reasons for the hope that lies within us, through Jesus Christ, our Savior and Lord.

Amen

7

The Importance of With

One Sunday, a woman visited the congregation where I serve. She sat alone and after the worship service I went to talk to her. She asked me about a member and seemed a bit puzzled. It turned out that someone in the congregation had mentioned the church to her and she had decided to come, but she had attended the first service and her friend usually came to second. While the visitor did attend church, she was obviously disappointed to not find her friend there. She did not leave her contact information and we have not seen her again.

A similar story happened when another congregant had mentioned the church and invited a friend to "try it some time." The week that the friend did visit, the person who had made the invitation was out of town on vacation. Again, the visitor was puzzled, alone, and disappointed. And again, they did not return.

People who don't attend church often don't know what happens inside the walls. They may have grown up in another tradition, not attended church for a long time, or have never attended worship before. Visitors aren't sure what to expect or what will be expected of them. They find churches to be a mystery—a place of the unknown. As a result, they naturally experience some anxiety about going to church for the first time. If people who attend our congregations are nervous about inviting others to join them, those who don't attend our congregations are equally nervous or afraid of what they might encounter if they do decide to come.

As the author of this book I can tell you that the first time I attended a Sunday worship service was as an adult in college. Two friends, Scott and John, attended worship every week. Almost every Saturday, they asked the same thing, "Dave, we're going to church. Would you like to come with us?" For several weeks I gave the same response, "No." And each time they responded with, "OK. Maybe next time." Next time finally came and I did go to church with them. Although I had no idea what was going to happen, being with friends whom I trusted and who could help me make sense of it was essential. In fact, had I gone alone (unlikely) I would almost certainly not have come back. But with someone I knew to accompany me, I started to regularly attend and it changed my life.

I am still grateful to Scott and John for their invitation to come to worship with them. I met my wife in church. I eventually became a pastor and began to work for the church. Almost nothing in my life today would be the same without that invitation from my friends to come to church with them. It changed the course of my life.

A few years ago, I was fortunate enough to be in the Baltimore area where Scott lives today. I called and invited him to have supper with me, where I got the chance to thank him for his invitation many years ago. I am deeply thankful for that chance to express thanks, and it was good for me to thank him and for him to be thanked. Otherwise, he wouldn't have known how much of an impact his invitation had made on my life.

In order for invitations to be received and accepted, it is crucial for members to be taught to invite people to come to worship with them. Remind congregants to offer to pick up friends from home, or to meet them in the church parking lot or at the main entrance. That way visitors won't walk in alone, which will lower anxiety and ensure them that they will not sit alone—they'll be seated with a friend.

A random invitation to attend church is a bit like saying, "We should get together for lunch sometime." We all know that "sometime" almost never comes. But a concrete invitation to attend worship "with you" can result in a visitor encountering the community of faith. So help your congregation invite others to attend worship by not only inviting them to come, but to come with them.

The work of equipping a congregation to be invitational is more than providing bullet points for what should be done. When done well, the ministry of equipping helps a congregation to envision, practice, and prepare to engage the ministry of invitation and sends them out with clear ideas of what to do and how to do it. Because many individuals don't easily envision what invitation could look like, it's helpful to provide clear suggestions and scenarios. With that in mind, let's look at a plan for helping those in your congregation imagine themselves inviting a friend to come to church with them.

First, members should assess which people in their lives they are likely to invite. For example, location is one area to consider. If someone lives in their neighborhood or close to home, a member can offer to pick him or her up and bring them to worship. In this case, the invitation might sound like this: "I'm going to worship this Sunday and I think you'd find being there to be a great experience. I usually go to the 8:30 service. I'd love to swing by your house and pick you up about 8:15. It would be great to have you with me."

An invitation like this is the most attractive. People know they will get a ride from a friend and walk in to a new place with a guide. Over the years I have had many visitors ask me questions that seem obvious to members, like, "Which door should I go in?" These are good reminders that newcomers are truly nervous about getting to church by themselves and feeling lost, lonely, or stupid. Offering a ride means you will do all the thinking and they will simply take your cues, right down to where you park the car!

If the potential visitor isn't reasonably close to where you live, then you may find picking them up to be impractical or even awkward. In this case an invitation might sound like this: "I think you'd love our church and find it to be a good experience. I'd love to have you come to worship with me this week. I attend the 10:30 service. How about I wait for you in the parking lot and meet you there at about 10:20? Then we can walk in and sit together in worship."

An invitation like this covers most of the key issues, although if they drive themselves they could still get cold feet and bail on the idea.

When a visitor comes to church with a member, having their host well equipped to guide a guest is helpful. Teach them to sit with their friend and explain what will happen, how to use a bulletin, the hymnal, or how the projection screen is used. During the service, being alert to if a guest is confused or lost can be a lifesaver. If there is communion, explaining how it is distributed can alleviate a key fear for many visitors. Members should offer to approach the altar in front of their guests and encourage them to "follow their lead." All of this will help make the first-time experience easier and more accessible.

After worship, it is helpful to introduce visitors to other members. There is nothing more difficult than working your way into someone else's small group, but if a visitor comes with a member, they have an ally to run interference. It is particularly helpful for members to connect with circles of friends at church, and to also bring guests into those same circles. In this way, guests come with you not only to worship, but also into social connections.

Finally, it may be helpful to encourage members to invite guests out to a meal before or after worship (If you go to a restaurant, remember to tip well. Wait staff report Sunday churchgoers tip lower than any other subgroup - not a good reputation to continue!). Mentioning breakfast or brunch in the original invitation can be an added feature that may encourage a friend to say "yes." This can be a great chance to spend time together, debrief the experience, and answer questions that may have come up during the service. Making the invitation one that includes a ride to church, time with a trusted friend in worship, and brunch, is a pretty attractive offer. Adding multiple layers of "with" to the invitation increases the number of ways that we can connect and encourage others to consider saying, "yes" to our invitation.

One other word is helpful. Remember that a vibrant church life includes more than Sunday worship. Perhaps there is a meaningful topic being discussed in adult education, or a guest speaker is coming for the education hour. This may be a chance to invite someone to an event that has more relevance or meaning to him or her. Perhaps the congregation is very involved in service, and a project or ongoing ministry has space for a visitor to participate in a meaningful way. In each case, the invitation is relevant and meaningful because of the activity being done together. Inviting someone to learn with you, enjoy something with you, or serve with you may not be a Sunday worship invitation, but it can be a great and meaningful starting point for connecting a friend with something that matters to you, to them, and to God.

For Reflection or Discussion

Scripture

Read Acts 8:26-40. The eunuch in this text has access to scripture but lacks the insight to understand how what he is reading makes sense. Philip comes along side of him and stands "with" the eunuch. How does the chance to come along side the eunuch change the outcome of this encounter? What does that tell you about the nature of ministry?

Questions

Take time to reflect on these individually in a journal if you are reading this book alone. Or, if you are reading this with a group, use the following questions to discuss what the people in your small group are thinking as a result of this chapter.

* As you read this chapter, what thoughts came to mind? What interested you most?

* Have you ever had to find or join a new congregation? What was the experience like? How did you first connect to people who were already there?

* Think about how visitors who come alone to your congregation experience the church. Do they tend to sit alone? Who talks to them? How do people in your congregation engage them? Roughly what percentage comes back long-term?

* Have you ever brought an unchurched person with you to the congregation where you now belong? If so, what was it like? If not, what has prevented you from doing it?

* Reflect on your relationships with people you know well. Which ones do or don't currently attend or participate in a congregation? Of the ones who don't participate, which one or two could you begin to pray about inviting?

Prayer

God of community, you have created us to live with each other rather than alone. Yet the pressures of life and the world in which we live often pressure us to be self-reliant and independent. Help us to value being with others and be willing to accompany them as they explore being a part of your church. We pray this in the name of your Son, Jesus Christ our Savior and Lord. Amen

8

Following Up

One of reasons that we invite people into the life of the church is that we hope they will discover that involvement in church inspires new life. Someone who only comes once does not make this discovery because finding new connections to God, new expressions of community, and new commitments is a long-term process.

As with every other part of this work, follow up is best done with intentionality. I have been fortunate enough to have someone attend something at our congregation and then run into them at the store the next week. It has been a great chance for a face-to-face conversation and to thank them for coming.

But it was just that, a great "chance." Although it did happen, I mention it here because I was struck by what an unexpected event the encounter was. And it has happened to me exactly once. It was not a way to ensure any ongoing connections with people. If all of our follow up were that unintentional, it would be safe to say that almost no one would receive any attention during the first week after his or her visit to our congregation.

This means that the church needs to provide an intentional way to ensure that guests are not taken for granted, but given care and attention after their first visit. This care can vary, but the following elements have been proven as essential:

A thank you letter from the pastor should be sent early in the week.

A handwritten thank you note from the person who invited the guest should also be sent.

A phone call or visit should also take place. In many settings, a phone call is better than a visit as it is less intrusive and still personal. A visit can follow the call to deepen the connections. This phone call can be from a well-trained layperson or the pastor.

An email message can be helpful. If possible, adding a visitor to your lists for ongoing info about the congregation may also be a way of keeping them informed about other chances to return. Be sure to honor ways to "unsubscribe" as you don't want the church to be viewed as unwanted spam.

A clear path to involvement and membership should be available and written in a clear and inviting form. This should include both clear elements of discipleship, spiritual growth and learning, as well as pathways to connection and belonging.

It is also important to remember that if someone returns, they still benefit from someone accompanying them. Coming back indicates they sensed something meaningful here. It is not a commitment to regularly attending!

So in addition to the things above for following up after a first visit, the following things are also important to consider every week. Many of these will impact the long-term experience for new people in ways that influence whether they feel alone and disconnected or beloved and connected.

Be sure things like refreshments and hospitality are available and accessible in visible and easy to access places. Many congregations have a coffee pot in the corner or refreshments in some other part of the building (like a fellowship hall on a different level). Easy access encourages people to stay and meet people. More difficult access means many will simply wander off.

Encourage people who have invited people to re-invite their guests to return. The concept of "with" is just as important during a time of transition until people know and are connected to other members of the church.

Teach people to watch for people who are alone and be intentional about befriending them. This can mean talking with new people instead of our long time friends. It can also mean connecting with a new person and then inviting them to come into our circle of friends.

Hold regular classes to introduce theology, practices, and ministries so new people can learn more about the faith that grounds your community. These are chances to invite people into concrete involvement in the life of the congregation. They are also chances for newcomers to articulate questions and learn how your congregation and faith tradition addresses them.

Celebrate the commitments of new people publicly when they happen. This allows new people's excitement about committing to a faith community to be seen by others. Excitement is contagious and also sparks the imagination of others who may wonder what next steps God is calling them to.

Invitation is the first step in a longer-term process of engaging new participants in a relationship with Christ, and following up after they visit is essential to building significant and life-changing connections that last. Inviting someone to attend or participate in something is the first step in a bigger invitation for someone. Ultimately, the hope is that many will become devoted followers of Jesus and find support and encouragement for their faith journey in the life of the church.

For Reflection or Discussion

Scripture

Read 2 Corinthians 8:10-11. Paul is urging people who started something previously to bring it to completion. We often include new people happenstance. How does this text make you think about follow up and the material in this chapter?

Questions

Take time to reflect on these individually in a journal if you are reading this book alone. Or, if you are reading this with a group, use the following questions to discuss what the people in your small group are thinking as a result of this chapter.

* What in this chapter stands out for you as most important?

* Which of the "week after" follow up things listed in this chapter happen with intentionality in your congregation? If you are not sure, how can you find out?

* Does your congregation have a clearly written and readily available piece that maps out a clear path to involvement and membership? How does a new person find out what being a part of your congregation looks like and how to take the next steps?

* Which of the ongoing and "every week" things does your congregation do well? If you could enhance one or more of these practices, which one would you target to improve first?

* This is the final chapter of this book. Reflecting back over reading this book, what is your overall assessment of where your congregation and its people are on the invitational journey? What step(s) would you like to see happen to be more effective at this?

* As you complete this book and reflecting on invitation, what excites you most about the chance to enhance the quality of this work in your congregation and in your personal life?

Prayer

Gracious God, you invite us to join with you in all that you do to bring forth the reign of God. We are thankful for the chance to be part of what you are doing. Give us eyes to see, hearts that care, and voices that speak graciously but confidently to the people in our lives. Help us to invite others to be part of your church. May it bring a word of love and a sense of meaning and purpose to the people in the world you love so much. We lift this to you in the name of your Son Jesus. Amen

Postlogue

Like any book on learning a skill or practice, reading the information is rarely enough to develop expertise. Even reading this and then discussing it in a group, generally a much better way to deepen the insights of any book like this, may not result in a change in the actual practices and behaviors of the people who read it.

There is much evidence to show that people who want to learn a new behavior or skill always do better if they don't just read about it. They develop ways to take what they are learning and put it into practice. This means that reading about becoming an invitational Christian does not mean that you will become one!

Therefore, changing the practices of our congregations collectively and our own practices individually requires more than a book alone can do. People need to be committed enough to this to build relationships and processes that reinforce this.

First, if you are an individual, find others to whom you can be accountable for inviting people and processing how those invitations went. Often, two people who are committed to the same thing can simply agree to meet on a regular basis and share how it went for them. Did they invite anyone? What was the resulting conversation like? Did someone come with them? What can they celebrate? What did they learn? What help would they appreciate? Each person sharing this with the other and then closing with prayer could be done once a month in less than an hour. But the results could be powerful.

Second, if you are a leader in a congregation, remember that practices matter collectively as well. Be sure to make the quality and missional clarity of your congregation's ministry a priority and keep it on the table often (always). Be sure to find ways to remind people, encourage people and equip people to invite on an ongoing basis. If you are the pastor, be sure to teach about this and include examples and encouragement in your sermons routinely. Also, be sure to have printed invitations, business cards, etc. made often and lifted up and given out for use. And see to it that your online presence is helpful and not a distraction. All of these things require regular attention. Changing the DNA of an organization takes persistence and time! But it rarely turns out better than the bar set by the leadership – do a good job here.

Third, in all of this, remember to pray for God's insights and blessings and remind the people around you to do the same. Vibrant spiritual lives marked by helpful spiritual practices are a sign of vitality and a way for the church to honor and lift up the God we meet in Jesus.

Finally, remember that it is a privilege to be involved in this work. This is God's work. The Spirit does the key work of inspiring faith – we are just invited to be an instrument through which the Spirit can work. Do not fall prey to the myth that you are the master of someone else's faith. You can be a helper. You can be a hindrance. But God is God and we are not. To be useful to God is a privilege and exciting.

So go have fun with this. Enjoy revisiting your congregation's ministry and your own personal faith. But always do so with the clear knowledge that as you work, you join with a God who is already at work. As you participate with God in that work, you may see and be a part of some amazing things.

About the Author

Dave Daubert is a second career pastor (previously he was an engineer) who has served in congregational, synodical and churchwide ministry positions. Today he is leads Day 8 Strategies, which works with congregations, judicatories and other faith-based organizations throughout the United States and Canada. He is one of the leading consultants for church leadership and renewal in mainline and progressive churches in North America.

Dave is a frequent keynote speaker, trainer and workshop presenter. He is the author of the books MetaMoments, Lutheran Trump Cards, Living Lutheran, Reclaiming the 'V' Word, and Seeing Through New Eyes as well as several articles appearing in Net Results, Emphasis, The Lutheran, and other publications.

In addition, he is pastor of Zion Lutheran Church in Elgin, IL where he lives and works with his wife Marlene (a social worker/rostered deacon at Zion Lutheran Church). They have a dog and two grown children.

You can find more about Dave's work by visiting the web site at www.Day8Strategies.com. There you will also see more information as well as other books and resources from Dave.